Pamela

while inspecting the infection
of a dying dog's eye
I see my reflection
in wintered gardens and polluted air

the snow falls (it jumps)
never with a scream
even when Heaven finds ground
silence

and you hold me
Good-bye my love, good-bye.

with the closing of an eye
we are gone

petals from a daffodil
logic and emotion
we remove them
one-by-one
wiping away tears

pirouetting on shards of glass
(lacking grace) we bleed

-

beneath the sky (animals hesitate)
whispering among themselves
The stars, they just are –
miles from it all.

ebbing stalking
searching and preying
for a gift to take
she opens her blouse
the wind exhales
we rejoice in our freedom
the decline before a fall

The stars, they just are –
miles from it all.

My dearest Pamela,
I am Paul

it may have been
(during a microburst)
a dandelion stood strong
with the weeds

my memory is flawed but true

within a womb of flesh and decision
an umbilical cord
a noose

I terminate my own birth
with exacting precision

a discord in my absolution
you pray for me

upon your lips mine I place
a sensation of us

breaking beer bottles
drinking whiskey with sin

the idle chatter
their words surround us
chaos and worship

it's a cold cold night
(at the equator)
a few degrees west of Eden

you take my hand

I am sorry for the words I spoke
and regretting the ones I did not
tasting the bite of your kiss

hold me, Pamela

psm (9-27-19)

Made in the USA
Columbia, SC
07 September 2020

19899831R00015